RuMi Art Design 2022

All materials contained in this book are the copyrighted property of RuMi Art Design. To reproduce, republish, post, modify, distribute or display material from this publication, you must first obtain permission from the author at:

RuMi Art Design
Email: rumiart@proton.me

Published by: RuMi Art Design
Distributed by: RuMi Art Design

Writing, Editing & Design by RuMi Art Design

ISBN 978-0-6455952-0-8

Scripture quotations taken from The Holy Bible, New International Version® NIV®
Copyright © 1973, 1978, 1984, 2011 by Biblica, Inc.
Used with permission. All rights reserved worldwide.

Scripture quotations taken from the (NASB®) New American Standard Bible®, Copyright © 1960, 1971, 1977, 1995, 2020 by The Lockman Foundation. Used by permission. All rights reserved. www.lockman.org

Scripture quotations marked (GNT) are from the Good News Translation in Today's English Version- Second Edition Copyright © 1992 by American Bible Society. Used by Permission.

Scripture quotations marked (NLT) are taken from the Holy Bible, New Living Translation, copyright ©1996, 2004, 2015 by Tyndale House Foundation. Used by permission of Tyndale House Publishers, Carol Stream, Illinois 60188. All rights reserved.

You know with all your heart and soul that not one of all the good promises the Lord your God gave you has failed. Every promise has been fulfilled, not one has failed.

Joshua 23:14 NIV

'For I know the plans that I have for you,' declares the Lord, 'plans for prosperity and not for disaster, to give you a future and a hope.' Jeremiah 29:11 NASB

May your Kingdom come soon.
May your will be done on earth,
as it is in heaven.
Matthew 6:10 NLT

Let me hear of your unfailing love each morning, for I am trusting you. Show me where to walk, for I give myself to you. Psalm 143:8 NLT

And I am certain that God, who began the good work within you, will continue his work until it is finally finished on the day when Christ Jesus returns. Philippians 1:6 NLT

Look! I stand at the door and knock. If you hear my voice and open the door, I will come in, and we will share a meal together as friends. Revelation 3:20 NLT

Each time he said, "My grace is all you need. My power works best in weakness." So now I am glad to boast about my weaknesses, so that the power of Christ can work through me. 2 Corinthians 12:9 NLT

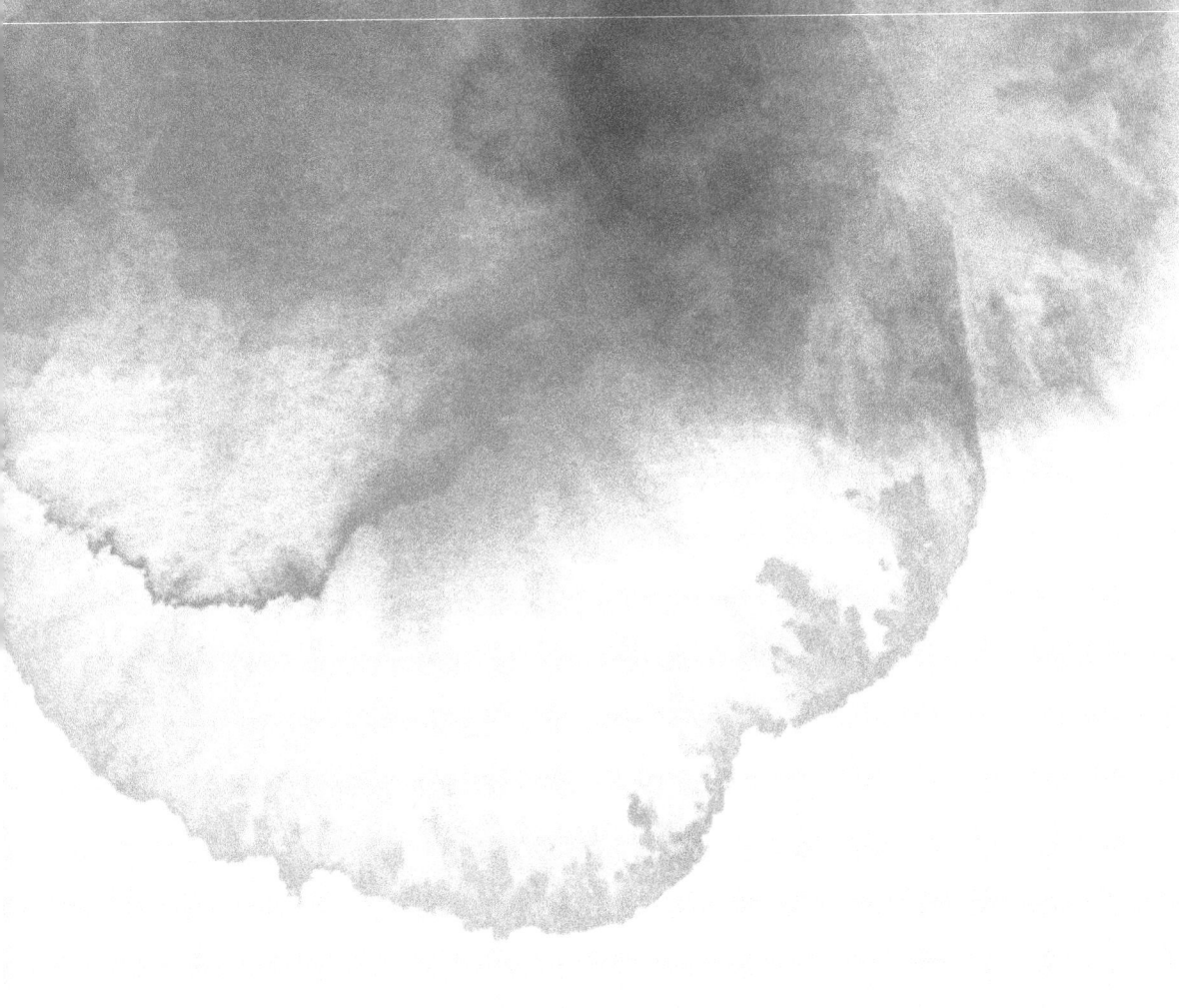

For all of God's promises have been fulfilled in Christ with a resounding "Yes!" And through Christ, our "Amen" (which means "Yes") ascends to God for his glory.
2 Corinthians 1:20 NLT

You will keep in perfect peace all who trust in you, all whose thoughts are fixed on you! Isaiah 26:3 NLT

You saw me before I was born. Every day of my life was recorded in your book. Every moment was laid out before a single day had passed. Psalm 139:16 NLT

Do not be afraid or discouraged, for the Lord will personally go ahead of you. He will be with you, he will neither fail you nor abandon you. Deuteronomy 31:8 NLT

Come close to God,
and God will come close to you.
James 4:8 NLT

Seek the Kingdom of God above all else, and live righteously, and he will give you everything you need. Matthew 6:33 NLT

For we are God's masterpiece. He has created us anew in Christ Jesus, so we can do the good things he planned for us long ago. Ephesians 2:10 NLT

But we all, with unveiled faces, looking as in a mirror at the glory of the Lord, are being transformed into the same image from glory to glory, just as from the Lord, the Spirit.
2 Corinthians 3:18 NASB

And you have done what you promised, for you are always true to your word.
Nehemiah 9:8 NLT

Then you will experience God's peace, which exceeds anything we can understand. His peace will guard your hearts and minds as you live in Christ Jesus. Philippians 4:7 NLT

And the Lord will continually guide you, and satisfy your desire in scorched places, and give strength to your bones, and you will be like a watered garden, and like a spring of water whose waters do not fail. Isaiah 58:11 NASB

He will feed his flock like a shepherd. He will carry the lambs in his arms, holding them close to his heart. He will gently lead the mother sheep with their young.
Isaiah 40:11 NLT

Yes, I am the vine, you are the branches. Those who remain in me, and I in them, will produce much fruit. For apart from me you can do nothing. John 15:5 NLT

> The Lord's unfailing love and mercy still continue. Fresh as the morning, as sure as the sunrise. Lamentations 3:22-23 GNT

For I am convinced that neither death nor life, neither angels nor demons, neither the present nor the future, nor any powers, neither height nor depth, nor anything else in all creation, will be able to separate us from the love of God that is in Christ Jesus our Lord. Romans 8:38-39 NIV

All living things look hopefully to you, and you give them food when they need it. You give them enough and satisfy the needs of all. Psalm 145:15-16 GNT

What an unhappy man I am! Who will rescue me from this body that is taking me to death? Thanks be to God, who does this through our Lord Jesus Christ!
Romans 7:24-25 GNT

The one who keeps God's commands lives in him, and he in them. And this is how we know that he lives in us: We know it by the Spirit he gave us. 1 John 3:24 NIV

But if we obey his word, we are the ones whose love for God has really been made perfect. This is how we can be sure that we are in union with God: if we say that we remain in union with God, we should live just as Jesus Christ did. 1 John 2:5-6 GNT

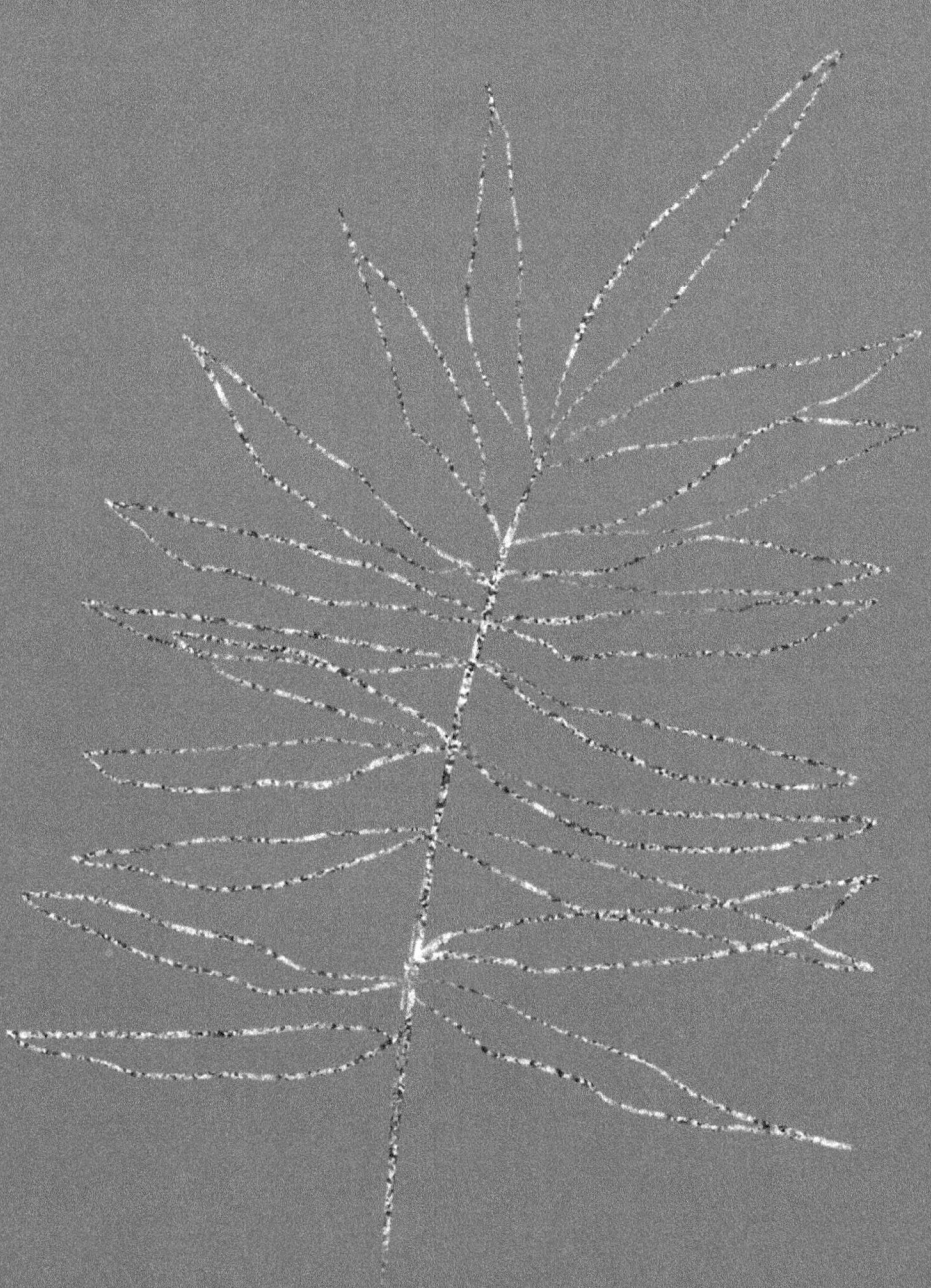

Do you not know? Have you not heard? The Everlasting God, the Lord, the Creator of the ends of the earth does not become weary or tired. His understanding is unsearchable.
Isaiah 40:28 NASB

"My thoughts," says the Lord, "are not like yours, and my ways are different from yours. As high as the heavens are above the earth, so high are my ways and thoughts above yours." Isaiah 55:8-9 GNT

See how much the Father has loved us! His love is so great that we are called God's children—and so, in fact, we are. This is why the world does not know us: it has not known God. 1 John 3:1 GNT

I wait patiently for God to save me, I depend on him alone. He alone protects and saves me, he is my defender, and I shall never be defeated.
Psalm 62:1-2 GNT

I am the good shepherd, the good shepherd lays down His life for the sheep. John 10:11 NASB

I will make you like a solid bronze wall as far as they are concerned. They will fight against you, but they will not defeat you. I will be with you to protect you and keep you safe. Jeremiah 15:20 GNT

*The righteous call to the Lord, and he listens,
he rescues them from all their troubles.
The Lord is near to those who are discouraged,
he saves those who have lost all hope.
Psalm 34:17-18 GNT*

But by the grace of God I am what I am, and his grace to me was not without effect.
1 Corinthians 15:10 NIV

Grow in the grace and knowledge of our Lord and Savior Jesus Christ. To Him be the glory, both now and to the day of eternity. Amen.
2 Peter 3:18 NASB

I am the Lord, the God of all mankind. Is anything too hard for me?
Jeremiah 32:27

I waited patiently for the Lord; he turned to me and heard my cry. He lifted me out of the slimy pit, out of the mud and mire; he set my feet on a rock and gave me a firm place to stand. Psalm 40:1-2 NIV

For God has said, "I will never leave you, I will never abandon you." Let us be bold, then, and say, "The Lord is my helper, I will not be afraid. What can anyone do to me?" Hebrews 13:5-6

He is so rich in kindness and grace that he purchased our freedom with the blood of his Son and forgave our sins. He has showered his kindness on us, along with all wisdom and understanding. Ephesians 1:7-8 NLT

Give me the desire to obey your laws rather than to get rich. Keep me from paying attention to what is worthless, be good to me, as you have promised.
Psalm 119:36-37 GNT

To give to those who mourn in Zion joy and gladness instead of grief, a song of praise instead of sorrow. They will be like trees that the Lord himself has planted. They will all do what is right, and God will be praised for what he has done.

Isaiah 61:3 GNT

The Lord will also be a stronghold for the oppressed, a stronghold in times of trouble, and those who know Your name will put their trust in You, for You, Lord, have not abandoned those who seek You. Psalm 9:9-10 NASB

If we confess our sins, he is faithful and just and will forgive us our sins and purify us from all unrighteousness. 1 John 1:9 NIV

Yet the Lord longs to be gracious to you, therefore he will rise up to show you compassion. For the Lord is a God of justice. Blessed are all who wait for him! Isaiah 30:18 NIV

Whoever goes to the Lord for safety, whoever remains under the protection of the Almighty, can say to him., "You are my defender and protector. You are my God, in you I trust." Psalm 91:1-2 GNT

Praise the Lord, all nations; sing His praises, all peoples! For His mercy toward us is great, and the truth of the Lord is everlasting. Praise the Lord! Psalm 117:1, 2 NASB

Stop striving and know that I am God, I will be exalted among the nations, I will be exalted on the earth. Psalm 46:10 NASB

And we know that God causes all things to work together for good to those who love God, to those who are called according to His purpose. Romans 8:28 NASB

Look up at the sky! Who created the stars you see? The one who leads them out like an army, he knows how many there are and calls each one by name! His power is so great— not one of them is ever missing! Isaiah 40:26 GNT

Come to Me, all who are weary and burdened, and I will give you rest. Take My yoke upon you and learn from Me, for I am gentle and humble in heart, and you will find rest for your souls. Matthew 11:28-29 NASB

You did not choose me, but I chose you and appointed you so that you might go and bear fruit—fruit that will last—and so that whatever you ask in my name the Father will give you. John 15:16 NIV

And Christ himself is the means by which our sins are forgiven, and not our sins only, but also the sins of everyone. 1 John 2:2 GNT

The Lord delights in those who fear him, who put their hope in his unfailing love. Psalm 147:11 NIV

Therefore, if anyone is in Christ, the new creation has come: The old has gone, the new is here! 2 Corinthians 5:17 NIV

Praise the Lord, my soul, and do not forget how kind he is. He forgives all my sins and heals all my diseases. Psalm 103:2-3 GNT

I will give you a new heart and put a new spirit in you, I will remove from you your heart of stone and give you a heart of flesh. Ezekiel 36:26 NIV

I am God and always will be. No one can escape from my power, no one can change what I do. Isaiah 43.13 GNT

"And I will be a father to you, and you shall be sons and daughters to Me,'" Says the Lord Almighty. 2 Corinthians 6:18 NASB

Praise be to the God and Father of our Lord Jesus Christ! In his great mercy he has given us new birth into a living hope through the resurrection of Jesus Christ from the dead, and into an inheritance that can never perish, spoil or fade. This inheritance is kept in heaven for you. 1 Peter 1:3-4 NIV

You make known to me the path of life, you will fill me with joy in your presence, with eternal pleasures at your right hand. Psalm 16:11 NIV

More than that, I count all things to be loss in view of the surpassing value of knowing Christ Jesus my Lord. Philippians 3:8 NASB

Make me know Your ways, Lord, teach me Your paths. Lead me in Your truth and teach me, for You are the God of my salvation, for You I wait all the day. Psalm 25:3-5 NASB

Look at the birds: they do not plant seeds, gather a harvest and put it in barns, yet your Father in heaven takes care of them. Aren't you worth much more than birds? Matthew 6:26 GNT

The heavens tell of the glory of God,
And their expanse declares the work of His hands.
Psalm 19:1 NASB

Humble yourselves before the Lord, and he will lift you up.
James 4:10 NIV

The Lord God is my strength, and He has made my feet like deer's feet, and has me walk on my high places. Habakkuk 3:19 NASB

I will raise my eyes to the mountains, from where will my help come? My help comes from the Lord, who made heaven and earth. Psalm 121:1-2 NASB

But from there you will seek the Lord your God, and you will find Him if you search for Him with all your heart and all your soul. Deuteronomy 4:29 NASB

We are made right with God by placing our faith in Jesus Christ. And this is true for everyone who believes, no matter who we are. Romans 3:22 NLT

God is always at work in you to make you willing and able to obey his own purpose.
Philippians 2:13 GNT

Therefore humble yourselves under the mighty hand of God, so that He may exalt you at the proper time, having cast all your anxiety on Him, because He cares about you. 1 Peter 5:6-7

Whoever drinks the water I give them will never thirst. Indeed, the water I give them will become in them a spring of water welling up to eternal life. John 4:14 NIV

As a father has compassion on his children, so the Lord has compassion on those who fear him, for he knows how we are formed, he remembers that we are dust. Psalm 103:13-14 NIV

The Spirit makes you God's children, and by the Spirit's power we cry out to God, "Father! my Father!" God's Spirit joins himself to our spirits to declare that we are God's children. Romans 8:15-16 GNT

You have searched me, Lord, and you know me. You know when I sit and when I rise, you perceive my thoughts from afar. Psalm 139:1-2 NIV

And he passed in front of Moses, proclaiming, "The Lord, the Lord, the compassionate and gracious God, slow to anger, abounding in love and faithfulness." Exodus 34:6 NIV

Wait for the Lord, be strong and let your heart take courage, yes, wait for the Lord.
Psalm 27:14 NASB

He who was seated on the throne said, "I am making everything new!"
Revelation 21:5 NIV

Whom have I in heaven but you?
I desire you more than anything on earth.
My health may fail, and my spirit may grow weak,
but God remains the strength of my heart,
he is mine forever. Psalm 73:25-26 NLT

He will cover you with his feathers. He will shelter you with his wings. His faithful promises are your armour and protection. Psalm 91:4 NLT

"Blessed rather are those who hear the word of God and obey it."
Luke 11:28 NIV

'Not by might nor by power, but by My Spirit,' says the Lord of armies.
Zechariah 4:6 NASB

Your word, Lord, is eternal, it stands firm in the heavens.
Your faithfulness continues through all generations, you established
the earth, and it endures. Psalm 119:89-90 NIV

God decided in advance to adopt us into his own family by bringing us to himself through Jesus Christ. This is what he wanted to do, and it gave him great pleasure. Ephesians 1:5 NLT

Jesus Christ is the same yesterday and today, and forever.
Hebrews 13:8 NASB

For nothing will be impossible with God. Luke 1:37 NASB

Therefore, everyone who hears these words of Mine, and acts on them, will be like a wise man who built his house on the rock. Matthew 7:24 NASB

Trust in the Lord with all your heart and lean not on your own understanding, in all your ways submit to him, and he will make your paths straight. Proverbs 3:5-6

He stores up sound wisdom for the upright, He is a shield to those who walk in integrity, guarding the paths of justice, and He watches over the way of His godly ones.

Proverbs 2:7-8 NASB

The Lord is good to all, he has compassion on all he has made. Psalm 145:9 NIV

I am leaving you with a gift—peace of mind and heart. And the peace I give is a gift the world cannot give. So don't be troubled or afraid. John 14:27 NLT

www.ingramcontent.com/pod-product-compliance
Lightning Source LLC
Chambersburg PA
CBHW040117170426

42811CB00123B/1438